LIVING WITH NATURE

LIVING WITH NATURE

Decorating with the Rhythms
of the Seasons

MARIE MASUREEL

New York · Paris · London · Milan

TABLE OF CONTENTS

A book for a more beautiful world

In my cookery books, I attach importance not only to what we eat, but also to the plates on which we present the food. This attention also extends to accessories such as cutlery and napkins, to the table setting and to styling in general. This explains the many interfaces between my work and that of Marie Masureel, whose projects I have known for many years. I admire her creativity and the way she achieves great results with simple and original props, which she often finds in nature or buys during her travels. Authenticity, harmony, and pure beauty are the main features of her work. The fact that she is now making her vision and way of working available to readers through this wonderful book will fill many lifestyle enthusiasts with gratitude. Not only can readers enjoy the unique pieces—real works of art—that Marie Masureel produces in her own home, but also the useful tips and reflections to get you started on making your own.

Marie is one of the few stylists to have developed her own recognizable style. Styling is, of course, not an autonomous art form. Styling is functional, serving to make our lives more beautiful, to raise our experience of indoor life to a higher level, and to experience table moments with friends and loved ones in a more conscious and intense way. In this book, she invites us into her own home, which she decorates in various ways. Hers is an original and very personal approach. Not only do we learn what motivates and inspires a stylist, whom I would dare to call an artist in her field, we're also encouraged to apply her vision in our daily lives. I'm convinced that, with this book, Marie Masureel will make the world a more beautiful place.

Pascale

WELCOME INTO MY HOME

Let me take you into my home for a year, and show you how I adjust my indoor space to the rhythm of nature. You will notice that, depending on the time of year, I need to create a different atmosphere in the house. Often a few simple interventions are all that is needed to produce a certain effect.

Since my teens, I've been aware of how certain things set the atmosphere. I remember the fluorescent lighting in my grandparents' house, how unpleasant I found it, and how the whole room suddenly became ugly when the light was switched on. I love authentic objects with something special about them. I remember my first treasure hunts, in the attic of my grandfather's pigeon loft, looking for unique finds. Many years later, my grandmother went into a retirement home and all the grandchildren were given the opportunity to choose things she couldn't take with her. How I held back from claiming everything for myself, because she had so many beautiful things. I also remember a vacation in Provence a few years ago. How we carried away dozens of branches of driftwood from along the banks of the Rhône, and how the car was loaded down with logs. I remember another trip to Provence when we had to leave the children's travel cot behind because we'd bought too many things in the local antiques markets.

I'm constantly looking for beautiful things. Not only in stores, markets, or on websites, but also just along the roadside or in the woods. It's like I have a switch that cannot be turned off. I'm inspired by color combinations I see in nature: those of a pebble beach, wildflowers, or autumn leaves, but also by the weathered look of bark, the tranquility of a horizon . . .

Inspiration is everywhere. Nature is usually my mood board. It inspires me much more than any particular trend or fashion. I'm passionate about everything relating to living with style, so much so that a few years back I decided to make it my profession. Since then, I've worked as a stylist.

I like changing things in the house. An interior is an extension of yourself, and as my inner self evolves and changes, I want my home to reflect this process. Of course, this is usually limited to smaller changes. Walls are repainted and large furniture items are moved around less often. But that is no obstacle to creativity. Chair covers, accessories, crockery, candles, baskets . . . Change these for something new or place them somewhere else, and you can create a different atmosphere in your home.

"I'm not a writer.
But words and furniture
have a lot in common.
Both are inanimate.
They don't move
themselves,
yet they can move you."

—ROSE TARLOW

WHAT IS STYLING?

Styling is the bringing together in a particular composition of items that, through their color, shape, and material, contribute to the atmosphere you're aiming for. These are normally existing objects, as the intention isn't to create something new, as in pure design, but to create a certain atmosphere.

Leaving aside the common use of the term in the fashion sector, in my own sector (which is all about still lifes), styling takes various forms: interior styling, photo styling, food styling, table styling, bed styling, creastyling, and theme or event styling, with the prefix indicating each time what the styling applies to.

Creativity is important in styling, but styling is first and foremost about combining and arranging certain items in their own, original way. It doesn't necessarily require a glue gun or other crafting supplies. For a stylist, creativity is more important than skill. Nevertheless, I regularly do creastylings, which you will also find in this book. Creastyling isn't so much about the pleasure of putting something together, but rather about the final aesthetic effect. In other words: not the process, but the result.

Although a certain heirloom, a travel souvenir, or a children's drawing is often part of an interior, styling isn't about the emotional value of an object, but about the aesthetic value. At the same time, though, styling has a lot to do with emotions, since it seeks to evoke a certain feeling, such as serenity, romance, vacation, playfulness, intimacy, nostalgia, and so on.

The goal is therefore both emotional and aesthetic; it's about creating a balanced image that evokes a certain feeling.

In addition to creativity, a good eye for aesthetics is essential. Many people, nonprofessionals included, have a natural, well-developed sense of taste; they have a feeling for it. For those with less of a natural feeling about which combinations of colors and materials work together, or don't know how to start a setting, the following advice can help them on their way.

HOW DO YOU CREATE A STILL LIFE?

Before collecting specific pieces, it's a good idea to seek inspiration and make a mood board. This doesn't have to be a major exercise. Sometimes, a single image can already serve as a mood board.

Try to pull apart the inspiration photo(s): What exactly appeals to me? Why do I like this? Which factors determine this specific atmosphere? Which colors and materials appear in the mood board? What are the keywords with which I would describe this atmosphere? What feeling does it evoke in me?

You then work out the concept. Here is a checklist of things to consider:

——————————————

- *Is there a theme from which I want/have to start?*

- *What atmosphere do I want?*
  - *Light and sunny or dark and intimate?*
  - *Chic, romantic, sweet, tough, lived-in, artistic, nostalgic, tropical, or . . ?*

——————————————

- *Which style do I want?*
  - *Natural, nonchalant, not-too-perfect?*
  - *Structured?*
  - *Minimalist (less is more)?*
  - *Overloaded (more is more)?*

——————————————

- *How many and which colors will I use?*
  - *Monochrome, cheerfully multicolored, daring contrasts, or moody shades of one color?*
  - *Cold or warm palette?*
  - *With bright colors, pastel shades, neutral colors, retro colors, or aged country shades?*

——————————————

- *How do I build up the still life?*
  - *Choose the base and background.*
  - *Select the eye-catchers.*
  - *Look at the three dimensions: length, width, and height.*
  - *View the major axes and shapes: Are you going to work evenly, unevenly, symmetrically, or asymmetrically? And in terms of structure, will you be opting for a circle, oval, square, rectangle, line, or a playful shape?*

——————————————

- *If necessary, see which natural decoration fits with all this (fruit, vegetables, flowers, branches, plants, shells, feathers, forest finds).*

Once you've got this fixed in your mind's eye, and know what the concept looks like, it's important to stick to it, especially when you set out to collect things or go shopping. It's hard not to wander off your theme. As you search, you'll come across all sorts of other things that are often nice and beautiful but don't fit into the concept. Then you have to be strict and keep watch on the concept. The purer the concept, the more beautiful the end result.

"Whenever you are
creating beauty around
you, you are restoring
your own soul."

—ALICE WALKER

CYCLICAL STYLING

For me, designing an interior is a sort of cycle. I like to alternate, and the time when it starts to itch usually coincides with a change in nature. The change in temperature and vegetation, the different intensity of light; all that gets to me. My mood alters, and I feel the need to make changes, also indoors. To evolve indoors at the same pace with what is happening outdoors. I find it a bit strange that, in so many interiors, almost nothing happens right through the year, and then at the beginning of December a Christmas tree is suddenly placed there for a few weeks, but that's it. I myself regularly feel the desire to create a different atmosphere.

It's not that I want to get rid of my interior; I'm not tired of it for good. It has nothing to do with having purchased the wrong things, objects that I now regret having bought. I only experience a feeling that my interior no longer fits with the flow of nature and the seasons. Compare it with a wardrobe. You don't throw out your favorite summer dress because winter is approaching; you just put it away temporarily because it no longer matches the time of year. The color, the material, the print; they just don't feel right anymore. But you don't want to lose it for good, because you know that in a few months' time the dress will be right again. That's exactly how I react with my interior. I put some things away, and sometime later my impulse tells me to bring them out again, often at the same time of year. The interior varies, but largely repeats itself year after year in a cyclical way.

Of course, you can alternate as often as you want. Having one summer and one winter interior could be perfect, just like you have a summer and a winter wardrobe. Depending on the time and budget you want to devote to it, you can choose what you adjust. This book does no more than give ideas. Its intention is to inspire. Decorating a home needs to be a good way to spend time, not something you force yourself to do. A simple fresh spring bouquet is often enough to bring a different atmosphere into a room. Or new candles and napkins on the table. Other bedding, a few decorative pillows in a new accent color . . . there are plenty of options with which to alternate and keep things lively.

You can also start slowly, and systematically build up a cyclical system of decoration. For example, purchasing new items year after year, or starting from one accent color and adding another accent color over time. Cyclical design has the advantage of allowing you to build up your interior over the years. You can save up and add items each time round. Many people already do this with Christmas decorations, buying new pieces from time to time without disposing of the old ones. Every year, when the time comes to immerse the interior in the holiday spirit, the same objects are brought down from the attic and at times supplemented with some new purchases. I do that too, but several times a year, not just at Christmas.

Another advantage of cyclical styling is that you won't easily get tired of your things. Once you're bored with them, you change them, and after a certain time you bring them out again from the cupboard or the attic. Often, you get back that same feeling of love at first sight as when you first bought them. In this way, you rediscover your own things and appreciate what you already have, and your interior remains lively.

Over the years, I've noticed that this way of living, with a cyclical approach to design, benefits from one crucial factor (in addition to sufficient storage space): a neutral basis.

A NEUTRAL BASIS

The term "neutral basis" appears frequently in this book, because it's almost impossible to emphasize just how essential it is. A neutral basis is the starting point; it's something you have to bear in mind from the start when building or renovating. Compare a room to a box full of objects. What's inside the box is the decoration, also called styling, whereas the box itself is the basis. Ceiling, floor, and walls are semi-permanent. Of course you can always break out a floor or pour a new one on top, but it's immediately a major job to repaint a ceiling or to re-decorate walls. That's not the sort of job you do six times a year, but you can perfectly well restyle several times a year. So make sure that the box—that is, the basis—is neutral, then you can go in all directions in terms of decorating, and can alternate stylings much more easily.

Most people pay too little attention to the basis. Not only is not enough attention paid to it, but often too small a part of the budget. It's better to go for your dream floor right from the start than to skimp on it and install a cheap, ugly, or temporary floor and then spend your budget on beautiful furniture and accessories. The basis has the quality of reflecting everything that comes up against it. To put it simply: beautiful furniture on an ugly floor gives you an ugly interior. We always look at the total picture, and because of the ugly floor we no longer see the beauty of what is beautiful. A floor is very important because, wherever you are in the room, you're confronted with it. In addition, it's a major job to replace it later. Indeed many people so dread the exercise that they then learn to live with their ugly floors. Setting the right priorities from the start is therefore crucial for the final result. Styling is all about evoking an atmosphere, embellishing, but has nothing to do with the basis. You can't correct a wrong basis with styling.

What is a neutral basis? It comes down to weighing colors, proportions, and materials to arrive at a result that you can use in many directions, that is beautiful in every season, and that feels pleasant. In other words, not too pronounced. If you decide to cover the walls with a wallpaper in a busy print and bright colors, then that can be very beautiful, but you're also nailing yourself down. Everything you subsequently introduce into that interior has to match the wallpaper. Of course, you can always decide not to keep the basis neutral in every room.

Everyone unconsciously gets a certain feeling in a certain space. A neutral basis evokes a very balanced feeling, neither warm nor cold or leaning toward a distinct style. Balanced in terms of colors and materials. If you like to alternate regularly and, like me, live in a temperate climate, then you want a neutral starting point where you can work flexibly and still have the option to go in all directions. For me, personally, that means walls and ceiling in light colors, combined with a floor that in some rooms consists of a graying parquet, and in other rooms a light-colored, matte cast floor. For me, that basis is an ideal starting point for designing my spaces to my taste in a flexible way.

Some styles lack a neutral basis. The baroque of Parisian hotels for example. At times, I find such interiors really beautiful. A daring "more is more" interior is fabulously beautiful during the Christmas season. You can wallow in the pleasure of the deep colors, home fragrances, wall tapestries, heavy fabric curtains, variously patterned wall-to-wall carpeting, and finely worked plaster details. But when it's eighty-five degrees outside in the summer, such interiors feel too oppressive for me. At that time of year I'd be glad for more oxygen and breathing space in the house, and to create a southern holiday feeling.

The disadvantage of a neutral basis is that there are some styles you can't develop in full. That's why it's important

to state that I don't develop complete decors. What you have here are just touches, hints, bits of a certain style. I keep my same basis all year round; but with additions in particular colors, shapes, and materials, I always evoke a changing atmosphere that matches a certain style and a certain period of the year. The intention is to show the many directions you can take with a neutral interior. Someone preferring to go all the way in one specific style will therefore probably find my way of designing insufficiently definitive.

In other words: a neutral basis isn't a must for a beautiful interior, but does offer a number of important advantages for people who like to change the way they decorate.

NATURAL

As an interior professional, people regularly ask me which is my preferred style. It can be difficult to answer this question, because it varies somewhat depending on the time of year. Yet there is one constant, overarching factor. I love natural materials and an interior that exudes tranquility. Designer brands and eloquent designer names speak little to me, though I certainly enjoy some designs and admire what certain interior professionals achieve. For me, the feeling of space is very important, along with a general sense of authenticity and well-being, of being completely at home. I've a weakness for weathered and well-used materials, and I generally find textures more important than colors. And finally, I love the countryside and for me, the interaction between my home, myself, and nature is essential.

In the past, I often answered "country style," but I've noticed that this term evokes associations in some people that are not or not entirely correct. The country-style spectrum is very broad and my taste is certainly that, but—for many people—"country style" means English cottage-style or Flemish pastorie style, but I've in mind

a much wider range of styles than just those. Sometimes I hear "I'm not so fond of country style, I prefer the Ibiza look," when, in fact, the typical Ibiza style is 100 percent country style. So there's some confusion here.

For me, "country" refers to interiors that are connected to nature, that have a strong indoors/outdoors interaction. Such interiors use lots of natural materials. This has the effect of blurring the boundary between the natural environment and the indoor environment. But a home or an apartment in a big city can also be furnished in a country style. These are interiors that make as little use as possible of plastics such as polypropylene, a material often used in designer furniture. A country interior will opt rather for wooden furniture and for natural fabrics such as cotton, wool, or linen, and not artificial fibers. In this way the country/natural spectrum exudes authenticity and tranquility, but exists in many traditional and contemporary styles. Six of these are discussed in this book.

Living connected with nature is very pleasant, relaxing, and even beneficial. At times we lose contact with nature. In these hectic, stressful times in which we scarcely any longer believe in religions or politicians, in which we're engulfed by stress and burnout, reconnecting with nature is often the foundation we need.

TIMES OF YEAR

In Belgium, the thermometer can rise to 85°F, but it can also go as low as 15°F. The temperate climate and the different seasons mean that nature is in constant evolution, and this forms the guideline for my interior changes. I view nature as a rich storehouse of creative potential; so much variety is possible. Just as nature is constantly changing, so does my interior. In other words, styling in rhythm with nature.

"Adopt the pace of nature,
her secret is patience."
–RALPH WALDO EMERSON

I've discovered for myself that, during the course of the year, there are about six moments when my mood changes, and I change things in the interior. Those moments don't quite coincide with the four meteorological changes of season, which is why I call them "times of year": early spring, spring, summer, Indian summer, autumn, and winter. If you follow the flow of nature, you can divide a year into six periods. I always choose a style from the national/natural spectrum that perfectly matches the particular time of year, for example the Mediterranean Ibiza boho style in the summer and the Scandinavian Nordic style in the winter. And each time it's a style that goes with a neutral basis. There's also one element attached to each of these times of year. I combine the four natural elements (fire, earth, water, air) with the five eastern elements, with which feng shui also works (fire, earth, water, wood, and metal). Since there are three overlaps, I have six in total, just like the number of times of year.

The times of year to which I link those elements sometimes differs from the traditional classifications. In Chinese philosophy, for example, the element of fire belongs to the summer, while I have it in the winter. I work from the interior point of view, and fire is usually more present indoors in winter than in summer, because then, we light fires in the hearth and place lots of candles. As this isn't an exact science, it seemed more logical to assign the elements to the times of year in this way.

Finally, I attach a material to each of those elements that I like using in my stylings. It's not that the materials are beautiful or used only at that particular time of year. Each material is one of my favorites and typical of my living style. Add up all six, and you have the ingredients for a tastefully decorated home that maintains a constant relationship with its natural environment.

The times of year	Element	Materials	Style
Early spring	Air	Spatiality	Nordic
Spring	Wood	Wood	Shabby chic
Summer	Water	Linen	Boho
Indian summer	Metal	Wrought iron	Flemish
Autumn	Earth	Lime paint	Wabi-sabi
Winter	Fire	Ceramics	Slow living

Of course, this isn't a strict division, because many materials are naturally bound to various elements. With wrought iron, for example, the elements metal and fire come together, because heat creates the ironwork. But the element earth is also involved, because the iron ores exist naturally in it.

All the elements are therefore inextricably linked. Not just in nature, but also in our interior decoration. An interior is always a combination of different materials.

TINNEKE VOS *is editor-in-chief of the Belgian interior magazine* Wonen Landelijke Stijl. *The country style has no secrets for her. She's convinced there's something country in each of us.*

"Country is corny? A bit passé? Forget it! The country style is more up-to-date than ever. This has to do with our current way of life. We live in a society where we have to perform more and more, and where stress is almost unavoidable. Not only do we want to build careers, we also want large families, to travel a lot, a nice house to which we frequently invite friends and family to dinner. In response to these busy lives we all lead, we want nothing more than to relax and enjoy the small things of life at home. That too impacts our interiors, where everything doesn't have to be that perfect anymore; some things can be a bit chipped or broken. This makes home a warm, cozy place to be. And how do you create that imperfection, that coziness and that warmth? You've got it: with natural materials such as wood, linen, natural stone, and wool. Typical country elements that we increasingly see in our interiors. Whether contemporary villa or a mansion, city-center townhouse or long-walled country farmhouse, the country style is so broad and accessible that it fits into any type of interior. In other words, there's something country in each of us. And with some, that might be a single vase or bowl, with others a little more. So is country really passé? Far from it!"

early spring

After the busy holiday festivities, we return to basics: minimalist and sober. Nature is at rest, so I make sure that my interior also radiates serenity. And that in turn ensures peace in my head. A new beginning. An empty, white sheet of paper. That's why, in early spring, I adopt a minimalist approach for my interior decoration, and I opt for light shades.

AIR

You often hear "tree out, plant in," which means you're supposed to place a houseplant on the spot where the Christmas tree stood. But that's certainly not a must. Let your interior breathe. An empty corner is permitted. In return you get oxygen and air. A wall doesn't have to be full of frames or mirrors, but can be beautiful in itself. No superfluities. No heaps of decorative cushions or knickknacks of every kind. No decorations, lacework, or embroidery. These only add a sense of heaviness to the look of the interior. Simplicity and clarity are the keywords. Everything must be aimed at maximizing the available space.

"January is my favorite month, when the light is plainest, least colored. And I like the feeling of beginnings."

—ANNE TRUITT

"Light and Space remind me of silence and emptiness. Very essential in a home. It's exactly like the clear silence immediately after a beautiful piece of music. Such empty moments are essential in order to process and respect all the beautiful things in life."

—AXEL VERVOORDT

- MATERIAL -

A FEELING OF SPACE

In contrast to the other materials we will be discussing in the coming chapters, a "feeling of space" isn't tangible. Space is all about a combination of light and air. Intangible and immaterial, but indispensable for shaping an interior and for creating atmosphere. Because no matter how beautiful the furniture, when you get a stuffy and narrow feeling in a room, a feeling of not being able to breathe, it's very unpleasant.

A few years ago, an international study surveyed the factors that make a home pleasant to live in. The study showed that—regardless of gender, age, style preference, and place of residence—we humans have a universal need for two things in order to feel good in a home: sufficient light and sufficient air. These are precisely the two factors that determine the sense of space. So space may not be touchable, but it's something we feel intensely. More than that: it's essential for our well-being.

Behind the mirrors in the bathroom is a storage cupboard, and to be honest it's a mess inside the cupboard. But because the cabinet is concealed in the wall, the bathroom still looks tidy. Additionally, the mirrors reflect the available light.

BUT HOW DO YOU CREATE THAT FEELING OF SPACE?

Imagine standing on the beach and looking out to sea, to the line in the distance where the sky and water meet. You naturally unwind. Because your eyes experience space and peace, you gain peace of mind. You can achieve the same effect in your home by giving your interior some breathing space. It's all about using a few important techniques to maximize the available space. Which is certainly wise, as building plots and residential units get smaller and smaller.

Create sight lines that are as long as possible. Don't overfill the space, and make sure that not everything is visible. Store things like toys in closed cupboards and not on open shelves. All these shapes and colors impact your system in different ways, with the result that—however tidy the house—you lack a calm view. Sophisticated custom-built furniture often looks calmer than a mixed bag of separate cupboards, dressers, and chests of drawers.

Work with only a few large eye-catchers instead of many small ones. This way, you lead the eye to one point, and the rest of the room looks open. Make sure you have large enough carpets: this is a rule that's almost always broken. A larger carpet has an optically magnifying effect. Use light colors. They reflect the light and that also gives you more sense of space.

Limit the wall decoration. A wall full of paintings, mirrors, and photo frames looks much busier and optically reduces your space. Underfloor heating is also a better choice than visible devices against the wall.

An undecorated wall doesn't have to be boring. In the far room, the wall is in Norwegian pine beams painted white, while the front room wall has been given a layer of microtopping, i.e. cement-based decorative plaster. This gives variety in the wall surfaces.

A large rug with a black-and-white graphic print, sheepskins, candles, and an armchair inspired by the famous Danish design. These elements immerse the living room in an instant Nordic atmosphere.

NORDIC

The living style that best fits the philosophy of this time of year is the Nordic style. This style revolves around the subdued tension between warm and cold elements that need each other to give the interior the perfect balance. And all this in a sober, natural setting in which space and light are central.

SOME CHARACTERISTICS OF THE NORDIC, OR SCANDI, STYLE:

light

Although the days are gradually getting longer, evening falls fast. That's why, as in Scandinavia, we have to cherish what scarce light there is, in particular indoors. The Nordic style glorifies light in all its facets, precisely because it's in short supply in the north. It's about optimizing what you have, even if that's not much. That's why lots of white is used in the Nordic style, because it's the color that best reflects light.

"Light is not so much something that reveals, as it is itself the revelation."

—JAMES TURRELL

contrast

Light also means shadow; day also means night. The Nordic style often uses a black-white contrast. That hard contrast is tempered here by the twig of green, the nonchalantly creased linen fabric, and by the matte tone of the black.

balance

The Scandinavian style is all about balance. Light counters dark. In addition, a balance must be sought between cool and warm. This is produced by combining cool shades such as gray blue with warm materials such as wood.

wood

Natural materials are part and parcel of the Scandinavian style. Wood is one of the most widely used materials here, especially light-colored woods like Norwegian pine or silver birch. Wood is used raw, in its natural form, but is also often painted white.

The combination of white with wood is typical of the Nordic style.

candlelight

The ubiquitous candlelight is also typical for this style. Until not so long ago, candles were the only source of light during the long, dark Scandinavian winter. You can imagine how many candles a typical Scandinavian family had in the house. Candles were necessary items, not luxury products. Perhaps that's why in Scandinavia they still use candlelight in a no-nonsense way. No multicolored, scented candles or rustic marbled ones, but simple, white candles, openly displayed. You'll rarely find a candle inside a protective glass cover, for example. A candle pan or a simple candlestick is enough. The essentials and no more.

skins

Skins are indispensable in a Scandinavian interior. I scatter them around, on the floor, draped over the wood basket, the back of an armchair in the seating area, or a wooden bench. You never have too many of them, and for the Nordic style, I use mainly sheepskins (both dark and white) and reindeer skins. The latter are rather delicate, as they can lose their hair if they dry out. Hang or lay them out occasionally in the bathroom; the steam helps keep them moist. Reindeer skins are best not used as rugs, because then the hairs break more quickly.

sober

Followers of the Scandinavian style are masters in creating minimalist still lifes. Even with a basis focused on a maximum sense of space, you can still add life and style to each corner of your home. A console, a windowsill, a side table . . . Despite the sobriety, the overall impression is one of a certain vigor. The trick isn't to overstyle, because then it becomes too much. Stop in time or even remove something. Less is more.

Consider carefully what you will and will not use,
because with a minimalist setting, everything must be
well considered. Choose your background and floor,
and then the eye-catcher. Lead the eye to one specific
point and ensure that the total picture radiates serenity.

FUNCTIONAL AND AESTHETIC

When thinking of Nordic table styling, forget Burgundian table scenes. Like the rest of the interior, dining is also very simple and minimal. In fact, all the general features of the Nordic style apply equally to table styling. Again, it's all about the game of contrasts and finding the balance between hot and cold. White and wood are also fixed ingredients.

In the Scandi style, we find few purely decorative elements. Flowers, yes, but otherwise functionality is paramount. Few decorative items—these are nonessentials and often add unnecessary weight to the interior, and stand in the way of an optimal sense of space.

Black and white, a game of contrasts.

Obviously, there's nothing wrong in surrounding yourself with beautiful things. The ultimate trick is to reconcile the functional with the aesthetic. No purely decorative items that serve only as decoration, but rather beautiful utensils. These are things we need every day, like a cutting board, scissors, an oven dish, or a fruit basket. When we ensure that these everyday things are not only functional but also have an attractive shape or finish, we enjoy them every day.

This is also good for the sense of space and for your budget, because if you have nice utensils, you don't have to spend money on extra items to make your house beautiful. What's already there—because it's in daily use—is already beautiful.

A tip here is to avoid plastics as much as possible and to choose utensils in natural materials such as glass, wood, earthenware, cane, or textile.

Kitchen linens, of course, have a practical use,
for example, for drying your hands. But they also
have a high decorative value in terms of colors
and motifs, breaking somewhat the neutral decor.

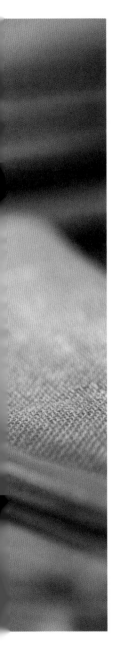

Ceramic items are an obvious example
of beautiful utensils. These sober,
white specimens fit perfectly into the
Nordic style, at once functional and
very pleasant to the eye.

VALENTINE'S DAY

We're slowly waking up out of our hibernation, but I'm happy for that to happen very gently. A good night's sleep, breakfast in bed, some reading. There's nothing better on a lazy Sunday morning or on Valentine's Day.

For the bed styling in early spring, I go for layers all the way. I opt for light, neutral colors such as white and pebble tones. The fabrics are warm and cozy. I love mixing rough and fine knits. Candles and lambskins are a must, and other indulgences such as a good book and a hot drink complete this wonderful moment of relaxation.

The layers of light colors provide a tone on tone effect. There are no contrasts, because the whole must continue to radiate tranquility. That's why I play—not with different colors, but with textures. The variety of coarse and fine is what makes this bed styling so fascinating.

TEATIME

During the coldest months of the year, I try to
be outside regularly. I don't make long trips, but
sometimes go out for smaller walks, especially
with our children. Then we pull on our boots and
don't mind if there are puddles. I'm guaranteed
to come home with some branches I like, or with
other nature finds.

To warm up again after such a walk, a hot drink
is ideal. A weak but determined sun, steam rising
from the teapot, a few skins thrown quickly on the
deck chairs . . . Even if just for afternoon tea, we
still enjoy the terrace.

Nature tells me which table setting to choose.
Steel-blue sky, cool air, and frosted branches
advise me to stick to cool tones. The reindeer
skin provides some comfort and warmth without
breaking the fresh color palette.

A cool palette: fresh metallics in
combination with green, gray,
and blue accents.

"The February sunshine steeps
your boughs and tints the buds
and swells the leaves within."

—WILLIAM C. BRYANT

spring

Nature resurrects; outside there's an explosion of green and a host of other colors. We're drawn outdoors, but I also start to itch to get started inside and change things, to follow the natural cadence of the seasons and bring nature indoors.

"The beautiful spring came, and when
Nature resumes her loveliness, the human
soul is apt to revive also."

—HARRIET ANN JACOBS

- ELEMENT -
WOOD

Once the sap starts rising, nature can be held back no longer. The blossoms bloom exuberantly, and trees that for months stood bald, subdued, and sometimes wasted away, now reclaim their place in the natural beauty of spring. Blossom-laden branches stand for new life, with which even the most exquisite floral wallpaper cannot compete.

WOOD

Wood is simply indispensable as a material in any home design that refers to nature. I'm crazy about it. Not only are much of my furniture and the floors in most of the rooms made of wood, I also live in a log building. Very pleasant and perfectly insulating, and also very atmospheric. But anyone living in a completely stone or brick house also has many opportunities to introduce wood. Some simple branches in a pot already do something to your interior.

When working with wood for a styling, I always think about which wood I'm going to use. About which type of wood, for example silver birch or oak, but also and especially about which color. Because there are a huge number of color shades depending on the type of wood. Wenge, walnut, oak, birch, elm . . . all have their own specific look. That's true if the wood is still unprocessed, but of course treatment with oils, stains, or lacquers can completely change the color. As a stylist, I naturally take this into account. For example, do I opt for a white-painted wooden floor, or grayed oak parquet?

And this relates not only to large elements such as floors or tabletops. Smaller surfaces like trays, cutting boards, and other wooden accessories all influence the final setting. Even wooden salad spoons need to be selected carefully. I choose between brown-black wenge, yellowish mango, and veined olive wood, depending on the effect I'm aiming for. I usually steer well clear of glossy wood that has been treated with high-gloss lacquer or nonmatte varnish.

Whether it's a large tabletop or a small bowl, wood invariably provides warmth in a setting.

SHABBY CHIC

In spring the flea markets come back to life after the winter break. I can no longer count the number of markets I've already scoured at home and abroad. Each time it's a treasure hunt. I love sniffing, guessing the history of a certain item. And then there's that feeling of going home with something special and then giving it a nice place. And where this unique item is peeling, rusted, or scratched, it only increases the charm.

The style I fall for during this period of the year is shabby chic. Nature shows itself at its most playful. There's gradually more color in the garden, and my interior follows that natural evolution. The neutral basis of early spring can remain, but I remove the typical Nordic elements like the reindeer skins and black accessories, and replace them with flea market items and spring flowers.

The seating area has not changed significantly compared to early spring. I've simply added some flea market items. Glass bottles, an old white footstool, and the wire chair in the foreground.

romantic

Shabby chic goes hand in hand with romance. The sweetness of outdoors, I repeat inside and on the terrace. Flowers, cross-stitches, crackled enamel, furniture with peeling paint . . . it's part of the casual and romantic style.

personality

Even though the way we build our houses is evolving and today's interiors look completely different from the past, vintage items and antique furniture are an effective way to make your interior more personal. These are old things that cannot be found everywhere or are sometimes rare, and that too makes your interior special.

A bunch of anemones in an enamel can: a typical shabby scene. To keep everything sober, I place no other flea market items near this still life.

nostalgia

Old, used things in the house have something familiar about them. They provide a homey atmosphere and remind me of days spent with my grandmother or of carefree childhood. I've a lot of things from my grandmother. As a teenager, I sometimes cajoled her into giving me things, and I still cherish all of them. I love old things. I also travel to Provence every year, where there's no shortage of flea and antiques markets. Such an antiques market is often educational for the children, and I like to surround myself with things that have a soul and a history. For me, there's also something beautiful in passing on cherished objects to the next generation.

dosing

The danger with flea market material is that it can be fussy if there's too much. I know many people like the typical Laura Ashley-style and traditional English cottages, but that's not the style I'm aiming for. I certainly like a touch of nostalgia and romance in the house, but I don't want to feel I'm living in a film set or in a museum. That's why I'm careful with antiques and flea market items: dosing and achieving the right balance is the message.

mix and match

The fact that your interior isn't purchased somewhere in a giant furniture warehouse or from a catalog as a finished set, but rather is the result of years of searching and bringing things together that are sometimes far apart in terms of geographical origin and period, creates a unique mix. Go by your feelings and prove that flea market doesn't have to mean old-fashioned. It's also a good idea to combine old and new. This way, you avoid the feeling that your entire interior dates from your grandmother's time.

One weathered old stool
next to the linen cupboard,
and the whole corner looks
special.

color

Blue, yellow, green, pink . . . these colors pop up in nature in the spring, and I therefore use them in my interior. Sometimes bleached by the sun, sometimes weathered and peeling from frequent use, creating the well-used look typical of the shabby-chic style.

well-worn effect

There are many painting and sanding techniques to give a piece of furniture a well-worn effect. I found the French curved-back chairs on a secondhand site. They were originally dark brown. I wanted them white and a little weathered, so I first applied some wax to the edges so that after painting them I could easily sand off some paint for a well-used look.

Layer on layer: first paint a layer in a dark color, then paint a light color over it, which you remove here and there with some sandpaper so that the dark background shows through.

upcycling

A glance in my scullery. Here we installed an antique bluestone sink that once served as a horse drinking trough. It's an example of upcycling, when you give a new function to something old. For example, I have a mirror in the children's bathroom, the frame of which was originally around a painting, but I no longer liked the painting. Instead of throwing everything away, I decided to keep the frame, paint it, and place mirror glass inside it. Upcycling is good for your creativity, the environment, and is also just plain fun.

THE GIRL'S ROOM

Spring has something girlish about it, with the pink fruit tree blossoms and magnolias bursting into bloom everywhere. It's also the period of spring celebrations, of weddings and flower girls. My daughter's bedroom is bathed in a shabby chic atmosphere. The eye-catcher is a metal bed crown that I bought from an antiques dealer in Provence years ago.

The linen bedding is a mix of soft pink, brick pink, light burgundy, and white. I've kept away from fuchsia and baby pink. Although the palette is definitely girlish, it doesn't look like a Barbie dollhouse's bedroom. I made sure that the shades were repeated elsewhere in the room.

STYLING
WITH FLOWERS

To play out the spring feeling in full, I like to use lots of flowers. The floral theme is also inextricably linked to the shabby-chic style. Personally, I prefer real flowers to floral wallpaper or floral curtains, because then my neutral basis will be compromised and I'll be unable to switch quickly to a different atmosphere in a few months' time. But anyone who wants to go all the way in shabby-chic style has to be serious about flowers.

I don't make complicated flower arrangements and I've never taken a flower-arranging course. To do something creative with flowers, you certainly don't need any special flower-arranging techniques. Nor do flowers have to be expensive. Many or few, picked, bought, or received as a gift—that doesn't matter at all, because flowers always immediately bring color and life into the home.

There are numerous options for working flowers into a styling. Very soberly, for example, to decorate a napkin, but you can also brighten up an entire corner with them.

Any time you have a mixed bouquet inside the house, there will always be flowers that wilt faster than others. If the remaining ones are too few to fill a large vase, then I happily transfer them into bottles. And you don't have to buy these specially: empty soda bottles are great for this.

At times there are sprigs in a wilted bouquet that you can dry and keep and then use as extra decoration, sliding them into a gift wrapping ribbon, or just sticking them on with washi tape as a playful detail.

Styling with flowers requires no special skills. However simple, it's essential for bringing the spring feeling into your home. A spring atmosphere simply begs for flowers. Certainly when the basis in the home is neutral, you need these sorts of things to create a different atmosphere. Flowers also play a crucial role in my Easter and Mother's Day stylings.

SPRING

- THEME STYLING -
EASTER

I enjoy working around a theme, and Easter is one of those recurring themes. I usually try to process a theme in a subtle, unflashy way, and with natural materials, of course. For me, the Easter table doesn't have to be in bright yellow and lime green, with rabbits and chicks à gogo. I don't really like figurines, which is why I prefer to work with branches, eggs, and flowers for Easter decoration.

A wooden tray on which I've placed a branch from a fruit tree. This was already mounted on a little base. I hung miniature glass vases on it and filled them with freesias and white daffodils. At the thrift store, I looked for some white egg cups and filled them with grape hyacinths. On a bed of moss, I placed quail eggs and a few egg-shaped candles.

The old enamel basin fits nicely into the shabby-chic style. I arranged some empty chicken and goose eggs on a layer of moss. Inside them I placed lovely pink and white spring flowers—violets, clematis, and wax flowers.

A small but nice homemade idea as an alternative to the kitschy Easter trees you so often see here. A twig of willow catkins with an egg hung on a string and filled with small white flowers.

EASTER

A table styling with a touch of the flea market. I used my grandmother's silver cutlery and festive glasses. Yet it's not a classically laid table, partly because the tablecloth isn't ironed. Nowadays it doesn't always have to be stiff, and—with stonewashed linen, for example—you can safely opt for the natural look. After all, the crease is specific to the material.

Otherwise, it's the flowers that especially stand out. I cut the heads of a few dozen "bridal crown" daffodils for a playful Easter table effect. They're an eye-catcher: remove the flowers, and the table suddenly looks quite bare.

MOTHER'S DAY

Roses and peonies are my favorite flowers, especially the white ones. My mother's name is Marie-Rose and my daughter Juliette Rose, and my wedding bouquet consisted of white roses. This makes them the perfect choice for a Mother's Day brunch.

Roses play the leading role in this styling. Not only did I put a lot of them in vases, they also inspired the other table decorations. White, green, and wood are the elements of this table styling. This way, the natural decoration—that is, the flowers—and the remaining decoration fit together perfectly.

This table styling was again given a touch of shabby chic: here I used old green bottles and a few plates with antique motifs. For the flowers, I chose ones from our rose tree that were almost losing their petals, for that "shabby" feeling. Because it's a climbing rose, the stems are twisted and uneven. Long-stemmed roses would be too stiff, and I'd rather evoke the atmosphere of romantic paintings of the past than of a tightly bound bouquet.

"A single flower he sent me, since we met. All tenderly his messenger he chose, Deep-hearted, pure, with scented dew still wet, One perfect rose."

—DOROTHY PARKER

The green isn't a bright grass green or lime green, but a slightly tempered green. The napkins, for example, are gray green and the glassware varies from light green to blue green. The wood as well has many yellow pigments in terms of color tone. Yellow, blue, and green always form a nice combination, since yellow and blue together form the color green. This way, you get a still life where everything melds together nicely.

- OUTDOOR STYLING -
NORTH SEA

After that long, cold period, spring draws us out of doors. The first chores have to be done in the garden; the children can play outside more often; and when the weather permits, we also eat outside. It's unfortunately still too early for evenings with long after-dinner conversations, but we can already enjoy the sunny moments, sheltered somewhat from the wind.

For this outdoor styling, I chose calm shades such as gray blue and sand, reminiscent of the North Sea. It seemed right to place the patio table next to a bed of long grasses, just like the marram grass that grows in the dunes. In this way, the background fits nicely with what's on the table.

"It was one of those March days when the sun shines hot and the wind blows cold; when it is summer in the light, and winter in the shade."

—CHARLES DICKENS

Tablecloth, place mats, or a table runner? And in which material? Cotton feels different from linen. These are things you need to consider when dressing a table, also outside. Styling an outdoor table is very similar to decorating a table inside, but you have to take the wind into account, for example, by placing the candles in wind protectors.

summer

Although I love every time of year, summer is perhaps my favorite season. Bicycle tours and walks, barbecues, picnics . . . It's a blissful period for enjoying the garden and receiving guests. On top of that, there's so much to style with: roadside flowers, shells, olive branches, lavender, driftwood, and much more.

"Life, now, was unfolding before me,
Constantly and visibly,
Like the flowers of summer that
drop fanlike petals on eternal soil."

—ROMAN PAYNE

WATER

Water is life. We cannot last long without it. Water is also essential for the flowers and plants in and around the house, especially in warm weather. We must use it sparingly, especially in the summer, because without water, there are no magnificent summer flowers.

- MATERIAL -
LINEN

"As long as the [River] Leie runs, as long as the fields bear the harvest of tough flax growing on its banks, as long as the dead flax returns to life in lace and collars, and blooms snow-white on the breasts of youth and beauty!"

–GUIDO GEZELLE

Linen is always one of the first materials that comes to mind for styling. I love the casual, natural look of linen napkins, tablecloths, and bedding. In my home, I also have linen curtains and seat covers; it really is a material that inspires me. I come from the region around the River Leie, known for its flax. As a child, I already loved the fields with their little blue flowers, but it was only later that I discovered the full beauty of what these plants produce: beautiful, powdery linen. Always elegant and also a cool material in the summer.

In the summer months, you need textiles adapted to the hot weather. Beach towels, hammam towels, thin bedsheets, picnic blankets . . . often used only at this time of year.

From origin to finished product: delicate blue-purple flax flowers and delicate linen.

SUMMER

IBIZA BOHO

A summery living style must be effortless and casual, because summer is primarily for enjoyment. At this time of year, I too am looking for that holiday feeling, a Mediterranean touch in the house. And at the same time, I want the interior to exude sophistication. As a matter of course, I end up with the authentic Ibiza boho–style.

SUMMER

LIVING WITH NATURE

You can express the Ibiza style without cluttering your home with dreamcatchers or buffalo skulls.

BUT THERE ARE A NUMBER OF TYPICAL CHARACTERISTICS YOU CAN INTEGRATE:

white

Ibiza is named "La isla blanca." White is therefore the basis for a boho interior in Ibiza style. Colors are permitted, but not on the walls. These are white, as are often the floors too. Colors are reserved for accessories such as pillows and rugs, which can have striking motifs. Often such brightly colored accessories draw on oriental inspiration, like kilim pillows with their typical, multicolored motifs. The bright, warm colors counterbalance the omnipresent white.

eastern influences

These influences are found not just in brightly colored items, but in neutral-colored ones as well. It's their materials and design that proclaim their oriental origin. Typical boho elements from Turkey are kilims and hemp textiles. The hemp patchwork carpets and cushions are very popular.

But lots of Ibiza-style things also hail from Morocco. Anyone shopping for boho often runs into the word "beldi." "Beldi" isn't a brand or material, but a Moroccan word that stands for "traditional and natural." Which goes perfectly with this style. Like beldi Berber carpets with their characteristic geometric patterns. The sheep's wool is knotted by hand by Beni Ouarain tribes, deep in the Atlas Mountains.

"Beldi" are also the hand-blown tea glasses with their typical shape and green color, and the Tamegroute pottery from the Moroccan village of the same name. All this is to this day manufactured in the traditional way, using crafts techniques passed from generation to generation.

You immediately get an oriental atmosphere with a flour-grinding table as a side table. The typical beldi tea glasses are hand-blown.

Tamegroute ceramics, named after the village of Tamegroute in southern Morocco, just before the Sahara. In Berber, "tamegroute" means "last place before the desert."

Finds from nature—such as shells, feathers, and a branch of driftwood—get a place in the house.

natural materials

Natural materials are inextricably part of the Ibiza style. Their appearance and texture make for a relaxed atmosphere. Natural materials appear in many styles, but in most cases in mechanically processed forms. The Ibiza boho–style, however, is top in terms of use of natural materials. On the island you'll find here and there items handcrafted from washed-up driftwood, feathers, pebbles and shells, and other items from nature. Casual, natural decoration is really essential in this style.

hippie culture

Ibiza is known as a hippie island, thanks to the hippie community that lived there, especially in the sixties and seventies. Many times you'll also find typical hippie elements in the Ibiza style, such as macramé plant hangers, crochet dreamcatchers with feathers and tie-dyed batik. Many of these are things you can easily make yourself.

stucco

Decorative plaster, polished concrete, Mortex, microtopping, lime cement . . . Lots of materials give a similar seamless, matte, slightly cloudy surface. Stucco walls, stairs, and floors are typical of Ibizan houses. Their origin can be found in tadelakt, a gloss plaster from Morocco based on lime and marble powder. During the drying process, the plaster is polished and then saturated with olive soap. The word "tadelakt" is Berber for "rubbing in." The result is a watertight plaster, ideal for wet areas.

neutral basis

This is the central theme of this book. Sometimes a few minor interventions are enough to immerse a room in a different atmosphere. By simply adding a single pronounced piece and some typical accessories, the dining area gets a different atmosphere. The Malawi cane chair on page 101 is a statement piece, a typical boho-style design that immediately becomes the eye-catcher in the kitchen. Otherwise, I've not changed anything essential. I just took some colored glasses and carafes from the cupboard, which immediately created a Mediterranean atmosphere.

This is only possible because of the neutral basis, which allows the room to be styled in a flexible way. The typical Ibiza combination of lots of white with natural materials provides in this way a perfect, neutral basis.

Among other things, I opted for microtopping in the bathroom. The effect of this technique is very similar to *tadelakt*. I love the liveliness that characterizes this type of stucco.

SUMMER

LIVING WITH NATURE

accent colors

Starting from a neutral basis, you can introduce one or more accent colors of your choice. You can even choose a different accent color for each room.

Some examples:

ORANGE ACCENT COLOR

GREEN ACCENT COLOR

In short, the Ibiza style is a mix of Mediterranean and Eastern, natural elements, and hippie culture. So many different ingredients to play with for a summer styling that mixes authentic pieces in a creative way. Because, as they sometimes say on the party island: "It's all in the mix!"

LOUNGING & SLEEPING

To evoke the holiday feeling or for siestas, you can put
in a daybed. Overnight guests can also sleep there. In
the summer months, we often have overnight guests.
Sometimes they sleep in a tent in the garden, but it's
also possible to sleep in a tent inside.

Pallets can come in handy here. This is how we magicked
a lounge corner into a sleeping place for overnight guests.

From lounge corner...

... to guest bed.

"The house shelters daydreaming, the house protects the dreamer, the house allows one to dream in peace."

—GASTON BACHELARD

ENTERTAINING

"We should do this more often," we say whenever we invite guests. We do it too little; we're so busy with work, the house, the children. Entertaining is fun, and whether you dine outside when the weather's nice, or you're forced to eat indoors because of the bad weather, it's always a moment to enjoy.

SOME TABLE STYLINGS TO INSPIRE YOU:

boho garden party

A boho garden party can be a colorful affair. For basic colors, I used a combination of ocher and mauve, but supplemented with blue, purple, green, and pink. With a mixed assortment of chairs, colored glass, and lots of wildflowers. All in the shade of the large oak trees in the garden.

And when we light the party lights and the candles, the mood gets even better.

SUMMER

formal occasions

On more formal occasions, I always use a tablecloth; it's the basis of your setting and it radiates cachet. Tablecloths are also great for changing colors from time to time or for masking an ugly table. Instead of a traditional tablecloth, you can also spread a sari or a plaid on the table.

an unexpected visit

"Are you at home? We're in the neighborhood and will pop in shortly." An unexpected visit? Quickly cut a branch of lavender or rosemary and you will immediately bring summer to the table. Little effort, and always beautiful.

SUMMER

barbecues

A summer barbecue is one of our favorites, and one of
the few times my husband also prepares food. I don't
know if it still has anything to do with primeval times,
but for me, firemaking has something masculine about
it. You can perfectly extend this to the table styling
by opting for somewhat more robust decoration. For
example, concrete and dark shades for the crockery and
replacing flowers with some herbs or an olive plant on
the table.

kids at the party

It's always nice to involve the children in receiving guests.
For example, have them make their own lemonade or
pick small bouquets that you put in a few glasses with
some stones in them.

sharing food

Whether it's an aperitif or well-filled tapas, snacks are always a party. The most practical way to do things is to put out little plates and bowls of different sizes. This way you can fill them to your heart's content and enjoy the pleasant social moment of sharing food.

in bad weather

In bad weather, we simply bring summer indoors: olive
branches, garlic, summer prints, beautiful glassware . . .
and the rain cannot harm us.

creative setting

If you like original table settings, you can make them yourself. I made spoons from driftwood and clay, and painted the dishes with indigo porcelain paint.

This styling is inspired by the Ibiza hippie culture, with the typical dip-dye and tie-dye, also called shibori. *These are traditional methods for coloring fabrics with indigo paint.*

extended dinners

The best part of summer entertaining is the long extended dinners. Together, just enjoying the delicious food, the setting sun, and each other's company.

"The summer night is like a perfection of thought."

—WALLACE STEVENS

Indian summer

Although it's still warm during the day, you feel that evenings are cooling quickly. The leaves of the trees change color, gradually nature becomes a colorful decor of golden yellow, rust hues, reddish brown, and purple. Although this period of the year is short and not a fully fledged season, it's received its own name in many countries.

L'été indien, Indian Summer,
Altweibersommer, Brittsommar, St. Luke's
little summer . . . All terms for the same
wonderful spectacle: summer displaying
its full splendor for the last time, before
fall takes over with autumn storms and
bleak winds.

"Summer is leaving silently. Much like
a traveler approaching the end of
an amazing journey."

—DARNELL LAMONT WALKER

- ELEMENT -
METAL

In terms of appearance, metal is the coldest of all elements. As such it provides a perfect counterpart to the color riot of late summer that already provides a lot of warmth. In fact, there are warm and cold metals (in the interior styling world we call them "metallics"). Copper, brass, gold, and bronze are warm metallics. Silver, nickel, zinc, and iron are cooler, and stainless steel is a cold metallic.

The use of particular metallics is subject to trends. A few years ago, we witnessed the sudden revival of copper. Since then, gold has come and gone, and increasingly we're seeing beautiful applications of brass; for example, in faucets and fittings. In this way, the use of metallics in interior design is changing.

Metal is an added value for interior decoration, capturing and reflecting light and able to spread a certain glow, depending on the degree of gloss and the color of the metal. It also exudes luxury, elegance, and power.

A green iron box, a wire basket, a planter in zinc, and a stainless-steel faucet. Styling with metals doesn't have to be cold. As long as you offset the "metallics" with warm elements such as wood, jute baskets, and linen pillows.

- MATERIAL -
WROUGHT IRON

In terms of mass, iron is the most widely found chemical element on earth. It's a very useful element, important not only in the construction of the Earth but also in keeping plants, people, and animals alive. Iron plays a role in plant photosynthesis and is an essential component of the hemoglobin used by red blood cells to carry oxygen throughout the body.

The working and shaping of iron started hundreds of years before the beginning of our era, in the Iron Age. From time immemorial, humans have used it to manufacture tools. It was forged—and still is today—into gates, table bases, stair railings, windows, door fittings, candlesticks and more. Both in and around the home, wrought iron appears everywhere. Wrought iron fits with any style: country, classical, modern, or industrial. It can be forged into any shape you want. Decorated or sleek and minimalist, wrought iron is very versatile.

Wrought iron is a combination of two elements that appear in this book: fire (see the chapter "Winter") and metal. There are still traditional blacksmiths who heat iron in a coal fire and then bend and hammer it into the right shape, but nowadays most metalwork is done by welding.

FLEMISH

Obviously, I cannot deny my roots, and so the Flemish
style is also discussed in this book. The Flemish country
style is both simple and at the same time radiates luxury.
Chic yet livable. Or more concretely: cozy, with quality
materials and an eye for comfort.

INDIAN SUMMER

cozy

Ask any Flemish person, whatever his tastes—country, modern, industrial, or classical—how he wants to live, and you'll always get the answer: "gezellig" (cozy). "Gezellig" is a term we use a lot. It refers to a pleasant, homey feeling of well-being.

An important aspect in creating this "gezellig" feeling in the home is lighting. In the Flemish style, the lighting is always warm, and usually indirect. Whereas in the Nordic style we often find a sober bulb dangling from an electrical wire; in the Flemish style things are more sophisticated and you'll rarely see the light source itself. In the Flemish style, interiors are bulging with mood lamps, usually with linen shades. The bigger, the better, because that shows cachet. Often, lampshades are mounted on vase table lamps or wooden baluster lamps, antique or otherwise.

Wall lighting is also a commonly used way to introduce coziness into an interior. Wall fixtures either have shades or they shine toward the wall or ceiling, creating a kind of light spot, which in turn—indirectly—lights up a room.

With lampshades and indirect lighting, you get a diffuse distribution of the light, which creates a cozy atmosphere.

high-quality materials

"The Fleming has a brick in his belly" is a well-known expression. Owning our own homes is very important for us, and we're ready to devote large sums of money for building and furnishing them. The Flemish style isn't in-your-face, but exudes sophistication and is chic in a discreet way. Nor does it come cheap, as the high-quality materials are expensive. But they are also reliable, and therefore last. This results in interiors that are more timeless than trendy, and more stylish than playful.

INDIAN SUMMER

FIVE MATERIALS THAT SHOULD NOT BE ABSENT
IN A FLEMISH STYLE INTERIOR:

OAK

The Flemish style is a warm style, and that's largely due to the use of wood, especially oak. A typical floor covering is a parquet floor in French oak, grayed with tinted oil. Oak is often also used for furniture and (ceiling) beams.

———————————————

LINEN

Flanders has been renowned since the Middle Ages for its high-quality linen. This is a material that must not be missing in a Flemish-style interior. It appears everywhere: table linen, bed and bath linen, window and seat covers. You usually find it in neutral tones such as white, ecru, taupe, or greige (gray + beige). The fabrics are usually plain, or with very subtle prints.
(See also the "Summer" chapter.)

———————————————

LIME PAINT

Powdery matte walls in—again—neutral tones form the perfect basis for a Flemish-style interior, characterized by few contrasts. The tones of the walls, floors, upholstery, and furniture all blend together seamlessly, for a highly harmonious effect. In a Flemish-style interior, there's nothing pushy—the whole radiates tranquility, starting with the walls.
(See also the "Autumn" chapter.)

BELGIAN BLUESTONE

Belgian bluestone, quarried in three main regions in Wallonia, is considered one of the best building materials in Europe. It's a compact limestone, formed by the collection of myriads of fossils in a carbon-rich mud. These fossils appear clearly as irregular white traces in the blue-gray matter. Bluestone is frequently used for doorsteps and windowsills, floors, countertops, and washbasins.

———————————————

WROUGHT IRON

This is the theme material of this chapter. Wrought iron is often combined with another material, for example, an atmosphere-producing lamp with a wrought-iron stand and a linen lampshade, or a coffee table with an oak top and a wrought-iron base. Wrought iron is also frequently used for windows and doors, both on the outside, and for glazed double doors between two rooms.

comfort

The Fleming is an enjoyer of life through and through. He loves the good things in life and is willing to work hard for them. He wants to see his hard work rewarded with good food and drink, with travel, and with an attractive home. Not in order to show off, but to live and enjoy comfortably.

LIVABLE-IN

In the Flemish style, aesthetics and comfort go hand in hand, because livability is important. "It's not a showroom," you'll often hear. The seating furniture here is a good example of this. The sofas are generously sized, sometimes oversized, with lots of cushions for support. They're comfortable and you sink into them wonderfully. Also typical is the loose linen cover, which—with its typical crease—looks less formal than solid upholstery. This creates a casual, lived-in look. It's also practical, because you can clean a removable cover. Good-looking and practical at the same time.

CUSTOM WORK

Sophisticated custom work is another example of the synergy between aesthetics and comfort. Many people still find a TV necessary in the living room, but they don't consider it visually attractive. For this reason, all kinds of custom-made solutions—panel doors, folding doors, or elevator systems—are used to ensure that the TV is out of sight when not being watched. That custom work is of course often in oak.

FAMILY KITCHEN

In my house, the kitchen is the space that perhaps best illustrates the Flemish style. It's a family kitchen. Much more goes on here than just preparing food. We do our household accounts here, the children do their homework, we watch TV, and receive guests. It's not without reason that the kitchen is called "the heart of the home." Since the role of the kitchen has shifted over the years from a purely practical space to a multifunctional living space, its design is aimed at presenting the practical elements in the most aesthetic way possible.

In my kitchen, we find a collection of all characteristic materials, and the focus is on the combination of the practical and the aesthetic. The stove is a retro gas one with a nostalgic, homey feel. The Belgian bluestone work surface runs through into the sinks. The full-length curtains are in linen and hang from wrought-iron curtain rods. The floor is subdivided into a cement-tiled section—very practical for the cooking area—and a section in oak parquet, which extends into the living room. All pots and pans and cookware are stored in custom-made oak cupboards. Finally, the indirect lighting of the wall fixtures, the mood lamps with shades, and the candles on the hanging wrought-iron platform provide a suitable atmosphere.

INDIAN SUMMER

Carrying over the colors and materials of the living room into the kitchen creates harmony and makes the home appear larger. A perfect example of how aesthetics and practicality combine in the Flemish style.

NATURE AS MOOD BOARD

The Flemish style is ideal for adding some spicy colors. The basis, characterized by lots of "neutrals," ensures that you can easily change the accent colors without immediately having to repaint and refurnish the entire house.

We often find, however, a certain reluctance to introduce colors into the home. How do you get started? Which colors and how many? Out of fear of getting it wrong and making the wrong purchases, people often end up sticking to their safe neutral tones.

Once you have firmly resolved to start working with color and break out of the cocoon of timeless beiges, off-white shades, and warm gray shades, then summer or late summer is the perfect moment. During this time of year, nature is full of color, which lowers the threshold because nature serves as a mood board.

The warm late-summer palette of colorful outdoor hues is therefore my mood board to bring some spice inside. I keep the ocher yellow of the summer and add red, purple, camel, and rust. I really love those colors, and they blend together very well. Out of practical and budgetary considerations, those intense accent colors are reserved for the accessories and not for the large surfaces such as the walls, or for large furniture items. Candles, branches and flowers, ceramics, plaids, decorative pillows . . . You have simply to immerse the accessories in a certain color scheme to create a totally different atmosphere in the room.

"Toute la vie sera pareille à ce matin aux couleurs de l'été indien." (All of life will be like this morning with its Indian summer colors.)

—JOE DASSIN

Red, rust, and purple. The outdoor palette is the mood board for the colors invoked indoors.

LAVISH TABLE

Mauve and purple are some of my favorite colors. Neither particularly masculine nor feminine, and evoking luxury, intelligence, magic, creativity, mystery, and spirituality, they combine well with many other hues.

Mauve and purple are rich colors that fit nicely with late summer, when there are also lots of them in the color riot of the leaves. From time to time I use this mauve table setting also as a basis for the Christmas festive table. Then, instead of combining it with pheasant feathers and leaves, I supplement the mauve with gold accents for a real party table, for example with gold-colored cutlery and gold-plated star-shaped candleholders.

With pheasant feathers and leaves . . . not only with the typical colors, but also with the natural decoration, I evoke the atmosphere of the moment in the table styling.

STYLING WITH VEGETABLES

Late summer is a time of exuberance. Deep, rich colors in the crowns of the trees, but also abundance in the fields. It's still harvesttime, and the crops are not only tasty, but also beautiful to style with.

In late summer, pumpkins appear at front doors everywhere. Pumpkins have long been associated with Halloween and celebrating the harvest season. I love the white and green-gray specimens, but they're a bit harder to find and often more expensive. You can also easily paint orange specimens with white lime paint for a nice matte result.

As well as the traditional pumpkin, there are plenty of other fruits and vegetables you can use for decorating, like apples, turnips, beets, onions, and artichokes.

"The perfect weather of Indian Summer lengthened and lingered, warm sunny days were followed by brisk nights with Halloween a presentiment in the air."

—WALLACE STEGNER

HARVESTTIME

Hanging lamps made from butternut squashes and tea lights in turnips.

Styling doesn't have to be an expensive exercise. With a few vegetables and a little creativity, you can quickly produce a stylish setting. I scooped out the vegetables with a wood drill and placed bicycle lamps inside the *butternut squashes before hanging them. I also placed tea lights into the purple turnips, arranging them among lots of other colored candles for a moody late-summer decor.*

CREATIVE TIP

INDIAN SUMMER

We don't, though, have to decorate with warm hues only. Gradually, fall is approaching, with its misty mornings and gray clouds. The combination of warm and fresh can be very pleasant in the late afternoon, when the sun starts to sink and spreads a golden glow. Here I added cool, gray-blue accents into a warm golden yellow decor.

"It was Indian Summer, a bluebird sort of day as we call it in the north, warm and sunny, without a breath of wind; the water was sky-blue, the shores a bank of solid gold."

—SIGURD F. OLSON

Gray hues of the oyster shells, crockery, and wood, combined with some blue touches in the upholstery and the blue thistles. These cool elements shine beautifully in the warm golden glow of the setting sun. And when night falls, the candles radiate a warm luminosity.

"Every leaf speaks bliss to me, fluttering from the autumn tree."

—EMILY BRÖNTE

autumn

And then, suddenly, everything falls silent, and nature
envelops itself in contemplative rest. All color disappears,
as do the birds, preferring the warm south. We remain
behind with remnants of what has been, with nothing new
on the horizon. Dead branches, biting gusts of wind, and
early nightfall. And yet this period, too, is superb in its
own unique way. Take time to listen to the wind and feel
the rain, but above all: to make your home cozy to counter
the autumn gloom.

- ELEMENT -
EARTH

Take a walk in the woods and look at the ground.
Everything that blows from the trees mixes with the
earth to form a fragrant, humus-like base of chestnuts,
nuts, leaves, and acorns.

Such a forest walk does one good. It causes you to
"earth," something seen as important in meditation
and energetic techniques. Earthing gives you energy
and firmness. Earthing imparts strength, bringing you
deeper into your own body and into closer contact with
yourself. It gives you the tools to get blocked energy
moving again, to discharge it, or transform it into a
constructive and positive creative charge. That's why it's
recommended to highly sensitive people.

Earthing isn't only done by embracing trees in the forest;
you can also do it at home, because home is of course,
also a place where you must be able to earth.

"Petrichor": the scent of
the earth after a rain
shower . . .

AUTUMN

AUTUMN

LIVING WITH NATURE

- MATERIAL -
LIME PAINT

The element earth gives us pigment powders of mineral origin, such as ocher and sienna. Pigment powders form the basis for lime paint. This matte paint is a typical material for a country, natural living style. Lime paint decorates the walls sublimely, turning the wall surface into a beautiful eye-catcher, with no need for additional decoration in the form of mirrors, photo frames, wall clocks, or paintings.

The matte beauty of this material is especially evident in deep earth tones. The darker the color, the more nuances that appear as lighter and darker stripes. Lime paint is applied with a wide block brush, usually with vertical brushstrokes, and it's those strokes that you continue to see in the end result.

The typical, streaked effect of lime paint from the brushstrokes during application.

To texture the lime paint even more, I like to mix other things with it, such as soil, extra slaked lime, and sand.

WABI-SABI

We're still a few weeks away from the kitsch and excess that accompany the Christmas season. I like to use this period—right when nature has come to rest outside—to decorate everything calmly and simply inside. Go with nature, don't resist it. The days are dark, so the house can also be dark inside. If you work with the right light and the right materials, it's not gloomy—just cozy and intimate. So few colors and few objects: well-considered pieces with a weathered look.

The style that fits perfectly with this is "wabi-sabi." It stands for the craving for nonartificiality, and seeing and cherishing the beauty of the imperfect. Originally it was a Japanese art of living characterized by purity and sober simplicity.

The wooden background is that of a built-in cabinet made of barnwood, that is, wood from old Canadian barns. After standing in the wind for decades, the wood has completely grayed and acquired a unique patina.

respect

Wabi-sabi is about modesty, about having an eye for the little things in life and appreciating them. It is about respecting nature, like discovering beauty in the unique shape and patina of a simple branch. Respect too for old age and transience, because something can become better with the passage of time. That's quite the opposite of our current throwaway society and the pursuit of the ideal of youth.

imperfection

In wabi-sabi this transience is allowed to show. No varnish, adornment, or decoration; everything remains in its natural state, even with peeling paint, scratches, stains, or cracks. Oxidation and traces of other natural aging processes don't have to be covered up. The object doesn't need to be perfect. More than that, it's precisely the imperfections that determine the appearance and character of things. The beauty lies in the imperfection.

It doesn't have to be perfect. That's quite a relief. In today's society our constant pursuit of perfection consumes energy and only causes frustration, stress, and burnouts. True perfection is an unachievable utopia. With the wabi-sabi style, things can be a bit more relaxed. So let go of that compulsion for perfection, just like the leaves that are letting go from the trees outside.

"The art of imperfect beauty is accepting the natural cycle of growth and decay."

—ARMIN FISCHER, DREIMETA DESIGN STUDIO

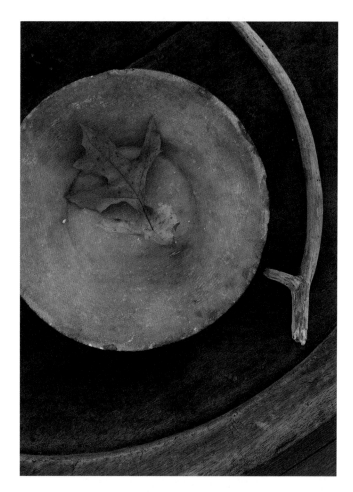

Collect what catches your eye and create your own minimalist *Wunderkammer*, full of finds from nature.

emptiness

Wabi-sabi is minimalist, because emptiness also has its place. "Less is more." Many people who like decorating fall into the trap of overstyling and filling everything too full. Stop on time: one object can be enough. This is how you keep it sober and pure, because in wabi-sabi the emptiness is just as important; indeed, even more important than the space that is occupied. But make sure that what you do place is totally correct in terms of what it radiates.

texture

Wabi-sabi being very minimalist, details are crucial. These are often found in the different textures of the materials used. A wabi-sabi interior is very tactile; you want to brush against it everywhere. There are not many colors, but all the more textures.

It's the textures that counter the void to a certain extent. A balance is created whereby the interior sometimes feels a little desolate, but never uncomfortable. The use of sufficient upholstery, which provides extra warmth in the interior, certainly also contributes to this.

With the pure, fully lived-out wabi-sabi style, the interior is reduced to the raw essence. A wabi-sabi interior is at times a bit desolate, but never uncomfortable.

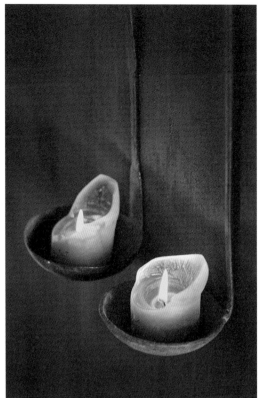

Some typical elements of my autumn interior: dark lime paint, handmade oriental pottery, rusted objects, and weathered wood.

Motifs are not a must. Plain upholstery is fine; if not, I would go for a graphic design rather than something figurative. Stripes rather than flowers, for example.

Attractive upholstery is one of the things that can give considerable added value to an interior. High-quality natural fabrics soften the appearance of a room and also offer an extra sense of comfort. It's pleasant to be supported by a few soft cushions, and you're guaranteed to get nice and warm under a thick, knitted plaid.

I like to use and mix different fabrics. This gives a feeling of luxury and of being pampered. In the fall I use furs, woolen plaids, kilims, alpaca cushions, and coarse linen. The alternation of textures provides an exciting setting. Certainly with few colors present, a multiplicity of textures prevents monotony.

Upholstery therefore provides something of a counterweight to the rest of the interior. The other materials—such as wood, metal, and stone—are, in fact, brutal and rugged, and so the upholstery adds sophistication to the whole.

Upholstery is also essential outdoors. Layers of plaids, fur, and pillows provide warmth and a moody outdoor feeling on the porch, a sheltered spot between the kitchen and the bay window of the living room. The large wreath of branches and roots is the central eye-catcher. To enhance its effect, I filled the ancient Chinese stone jars with two types of branches.

- CREASTYLING -
FOREST FINDS

Branches, chestnuts, acorns, nuts, leaves . . .
I head outdoors, returning home each time
with lots of forest finds. They're free and give
your interior a natural decor. You can of course
simply put them in a wooden bowl and it's
always beautiful, but you can also do
something creative with them.

CREATIVE TIP

*Bring the autumn theme to the table in a simple but
stylish way by stamping these black linen napkins. I
painted a fallen leaf with gold paint and carefully
pressed it onto the linen fabric so that the veins stand
out beautifully. I used the same leaf every time, but
you can also vary leaf types. This way you get different
shapes on your napkins.*

Cow parsnip has earned a permanent decoration place in many country interiors. It's best not to cut it in the summer, but wait until the autumn when it has dried, because otherwise you could get ugly burns. The dried branches are light and very easy to saw into pieces, or to cut in two with secateurs.

I produced a decorative ladder from two large cow parsnip stems. I also tied some stems together into a perfect vase for the dried rosehip branches still in the house. An original fall tablepiece that requires no water.

PURE & AUTHENTIC

In the wabi-sabi table styling, no oversized white nouvelle cuisine plates that look like meticulously styled miniature paintings. No junk or fatty foods, but casseroles and stews. Go for pure, genuine food such as organically grown vegetables and fair-trade products, which are selected and prepared with respect for nature, people, and their origins.

In addition to nonartificiality, austerity is a typical feature of the wabi-sabi style. So don't expect any Burgundian scenes. It's about creating a friendly, intimate atmosphere, and not an exuberant party mood. No fancy table setting in the separate dining room, but sitting cozily side by side at the kitchen table and afterward doing the dishes together.

A NUMBER OF TABLE AND FOOD STYLING TIPS
THAT GO WITH THIS WABI-SABI STYLE:

At this time of year, I like to use dark earthenware. I
love the tone-on-tone aspect of dark crockery on a
dark surface, such as my bluestone work surface or
a dark wood tabletop.

With a food styling using dark vegetables and fruits such
as salsify, black radish, or figs, this tone-on-tone effect
always looks very pleasant and natural. Which is why we
call this style of photography "dark and moody."

Dark and moody. The earthy tones of the mushrooms are reflected
in the background, for a still life in autumnal nuances.

Terracotta: literally "baked earth."

Authentic utensils, such as my collection of antique cutting boards and my grandmother's silver cutlery, are preferred. The traces of years of use are irresistibly beautiful to me. Brand-new items cannot match old ones. They are pure; memories of past life. They fill me with nostalgia and that's why I cherish them.

You don't have to be a good cook to make a tasty setting. The most important thing is the interaction between the food and the surface. Plastic of any kind is out of the question for this. Wood, natural stone, zinc, and concrete all work well here.

Disposable products like paper napkins don't fit into the wabi-sabi philosophy at all. That's why I use fabric ones.

I make sure that I also adjust the cutlery accordingly. For example, in a dark setting like this one, always opt for dark cutlery with preferably as little shine as possible. This may seem like overattention to details, but these are essential for the effect.

The wabi-sabi color palette is therefore often monochrome. A still life in a single color can be interesting, but then you have to focus on the shape of the objects and the play of materials. The pottery, the sheepskin, the wooden spoons, and the coffee beans are all brown, but in different materials. As such, they have different degrees of gloss, which means that the light is reflected differently. In terms of contours, the focus is on the two striking circles of the bowls. This gives a certain relief, in place of a vague brown mass.

HYGGE

Animals begin to hibernate and it's dark early. We're part of nature, which now takes a break before resetting. We humans need this break too. Go into hibernation a bit by opting for dark bedding. I chose wrinkled linen, supplementing it with lots of pillows, a bedspread, and a coarse-knit plaid. Work in layers for a real warm, nest-like feeling.

With light walls too, it's possible to create an intimate wabi-sabi style. You can use old shutters, door panels, a folding screen, or a dark painted canvas for this.

More hours of sleep are unfortunately not always possible, so try to pay attention to creating cozy rest moments in the house. There's nothing as wonderful as coming back to yourself in your comfortable cocoon after a long day's work.

The Danes have the perfect term for this: "hygge."

"Hygge" is best translated as "making things cozy and enjoying small things." Hygge fits perfectly with the wabi-sabi philosophy. Here, too, it's not about excess and luxury, but about staying close to yourself and nature, seeking peace and enjoying a hot drink, a good book, and a crackling fire. It's nesting, refueling energy in a pleasant environment with candles and plaids. But it can also be a cozy cheese and wine evening with your best friends, very pleasantly enjoying the atmosphere, the goodies on the table, and each other.

Although hygge is a relatively new concept in our part of the world and sounds trendy, it should certainly not remain something one-off. De-stressing isn't about one wellness afternoon every six months at the beauty farm. We need to incorporate it more and more into our daily rhythm.

We don't have to do it in spectacular ways. Call it "stolen moments of pleasure" or "daily wellness": take a moment to consciously enjoy a warm shower or a walk with the dog. For example, I also try to make moments to enjoy from time to time when I'm putting in long hours and working late on the computer. I light candles, make a hot chocolate with cinnamon, and turn on quiet music.

Hygge isn't about spectacular activities planned long in advance. It's more about stolen moments of deep and subdued pleasure.

"Hygge. Warm your heart, your body, and your soul."

TONE ON TONE

The smoke from the fires mixes with the mist. The silhouettes of chairs and table are almost indistinguishable from the branches of the trees. The darkly decorated table blends, as it were, into the natural setting and becomes one with the environment.

Candles, fire bowls, furs . . . all ways to make things comfortable and cozy outside. The dark crockery and the old, weathered folding table that once belonged to a market seller also extend the wabi-sabi details outdoors.

winter

Wintertime.
Cold outside, warm inside.
Winter is a time of silence. No birdsong, the snow
muffles all noise. A time for reflection and making
good resolutions.
Winter is also shouting with glee at the first snow, the rustle
of gift wrapping paper, and noisy fireworks at New Year.

In short, winter is a period of opposites. The primal version of the opposing cosmic forces is the Chinese yin and yang. Cold is associated with yin; heat with yang. But yin and yang are not merely opposites—they are first and foremost complementary values, interconnected as are also inside and outside. Nature connected with the interior.

"What good is the warmth of summer, without the cold of winter to give it sweetness?"

—JOHN STEINBECK

FIRE

Fire is one of the most powerful elements.
In feng shui—where this element is also used to
live optimally—it's sometimes advised to introduce
something red into the interior, because it's of course
a very fiery color. This isn't, however, a must. You can
also take "fire" literally and light lots of candles
and a fire.

"Winter is the time for comfort, good food, for warmth, for the touch of a friendly hand and a talk beside the fire, it is a time for home."

—EDITH SITWELL

I couldn't live without candles and an open fireplace. For me, they are really essential for making the house warm and cozy. Whichever your preferred living style—modern, rural, industrial, or classical—the universal desire is for coziness. Nobody ever says "I want to live in an uncozy house." Fire is very important for creating coziness.

When I arrive somewhere for the first time, I often look to see whether there are candles and whether the wicks are white or black. White wicks mean the candles have never been lit. Some people place candles, but don't use them; in particular, expensive candles. For me that's a shame, because the magic is only there when the candles are actually burning.

CERAMIC

Fire reminds me of ceramic, a material that traditionally requires fire and heat to make it. The clay is fired and something new is created.

With ceramic, two elements actually come together: earth and fire. According to Chinese philosophy, "Earth" belongs to yin, and "fire" to yang. Ceramic unites the two.

SLOW LIVING

We take stock of the past year. For some this provides the impetus to make New Year's resolutions. One good resolution may be to take things a bit easily, to focus more on what really counts, to consciously enjoy the small moments, of family and of being with people you like to see. Being satisfied with what you have—more doesn't always have to be better. Especially in this season of gifts, with wish lists and abundance, slow living is a healthy attitude.

"Nature does not hurry, yet everything is accomplished."

—LAO TSE

Slow living: stop time, be in the moment, and be satisfied.

WINTER

mindfulness

Slow living came in the aftermath of the slow food movement, and this in turn came as a counterreaction to fast food. Slow food is about going back to traditional products and consciously taking the time to cook and dine. Slow living is about taking time to live consciously. In other words: mindfulness. Focusing on what is really important and what makes you sincerely and intensely happy. Both revolve around authenticity and purity.

lagom

Hygge (see the chapter "Autumn") is certainly part of the slow-living philosophy, but slow living goes even further. There's another–this time Swedish–term that expresses it well:

Lagom
Not too little, not too much. But just right.

More and more people are realizing that the pendulum has swung too far. Status stress, traffic jams, lifestyle diseases . . .

While "hygge" is about a moment of the day, a stolen moment of pleasure, "lagom" is more a way of life. A lifestyle that focuses on sincerity, modesty, and balance. Hygge is about enjoying, lagom about learning to appreciate what you already have and being satisfied. Quality over quantity.

And that's not so easy. Because who isn't ambitious, and who isn't looking for the next interesting project? But occasionally we need to take some lagom into our lives and live a little more slowly, reflecting on what we already have and have already achieved, and being thankful for that. For me, that's nice. As the English say: "Count your blessings."

Slow living is therefore not just about relaxing, but also about slowing down, decluttering, and rediscovering.

This calls us to declutter the house, because we want clear minds to be able to relax and unwind, and that's difficult when there's too much all around you. When the interior is overflowing with accessories, collections, and toys, the furnishings sink into it and you no longer see the forest for the trees. That causes unrest. (See also the article on the feeling of space in the "Early Spring" chapter.)

Just like most other living styles in this book, slow living is all about "less is more." In the first instance it's all about reducing, ultimately in order to achieve more satisfaction. However, it's not about pure minimalism. After all, lagom also means "not too little," so you don't have to completely strip your home and live in a bare, empty environment. It's all about removing flotsam from the interior, making it a bit more manageable. But retain in particular what makes you happy and joyful, that which expresses your personality and creativity.

"Limit everything to the essential. But do not remove the poetry."

—DIETER RAMS

REDUCING IN FOUR STEPS:

CONSUMING LESS

Don't always be looking for "the next great thing" or the latest trend. That's not always easy in our overmarketed consumer society.

LESS STUFF

Review what you have and put away the things that don't offer you happiness. Got something as a gift that you actually don't like? Get rid of it. Something you brought back home from holiday but you've long been tired of or doesn't harmonize with the rest of your interior? Jettison it. Make someone else happy with it; for example, by taking it to the thrift store.

LESS ALL AT THE SAME TIME, ROTATE

Don't put out everything you have, just as you don't wear all your jewelry or scarves at once. Put a few things in boxes in the attic, then alternate in a few months' time. By then, you'll have forgotten that you had some of those things. You'll rediscover them, find a nice place for them in the house, and appreciate them again.

Rotating is a good method of reducing the number of objects, and creating some clarity in the interior, without throwing everything away. My mood changes with the seasons, so sometimes I want to replace something with something else. But that doesn't mean I'm tired of it and want to throw it out.

So I store it temporarily in a closet or in the attic. Sometimes I also rotate things from one room to another. For example, a Nordic or Ibiza style armchair stays in the living room or kitchen only during that specific period of the year. During the rest of the year, the same chair is placed more discreetly in one of the children's rooms or in the office. In other words, I rotate mainly statement pieces and distinctly styled accessories.

FEWER COLORS AND CONTRASTS

You don't necessarily have to minimize the number of items; you can also reduce the number of colors and contrasts. You then work with tone-on-tone decoration. The interior looks less cluttered as a result.

Tone on tone is best done with light tones: you introduce more light into your home, have a better overview, and therefore peace of mind. This makes the interior both warm and cozy, yet clearly defined. Again yin and yang. It's an in-between phase, between the dark, intimate, wabi-sabi style of fall and the bright Nordic style of early spring, which will arrive again in a few weeks. A mix of warm, fresh "neutrals": brown, gray, camel, beige, and clear white. I also use both light and dark wood during this period.

Light tone-on-tone styling
with plaids and skins.

CHRISTMAS AND NEW YEAR'S

It's no accident that ceramic is the theme material
for this chapter. Take out your most beautiful crockery,
because this time of year a lot of tables have to be styled.

Whether it's a formal setting or a cozy "winter wonderland" atmosphere, I always use beautiful ceramics, stylish table linen, and wooden accents, choosing cutlery and glassware in particular to create differences in atmosphere. Festive silver cutlery and classic wineglasses give the table a more formal look.

"Luxury to me is not about buying expensive things; it's about living in a way where you appreciate things."

—OSCAR DE LA RENTA

CHRISTMAS AT HOME

Decluttering may sound contradictory for the end-of-year period, with often ornate Christmas decorations and festively decorated tables. I therefore opt for a natural holiday, one that is never over the top. I don't like kitschy Christmases, but I do like them to be cozy and warm. So I don't exaggerate with my decorations, and above all make sure that the extra decorations I put up for Christmas also fit in with the rest of the decor. Many people place just a tree, but I like to put Christmas touches everywhere in the house. This way the decoration really blends into the interior, rather than having a single–sometimes far too loud–eye-catcher.

It doesn't always have to be a large Christmas tree; a few branches can already be enough to convey the holiday feeling. I also alternate the decorations in the tree. Sometimes I just hang lights in the tree, and I put the balls in a bowl or as decoration on the party table. If an ornament smashes to the floor, I keep the shards for the Christmas party and sprinkle them on the table-cloth as glitter.

- CREASTYLING -
CHRISTMAS DECORATION

In this time of excess, slow living means that the house
should not be dripping with kitsch. You can make
decorations yourself with natural materials. For example,
I love the combination of clay, branches, and linen.

CLAY

Clay is the easy DIY version of ceramic. For the clay creations, you can use normal white, air-drying clay, because obviously not everyone has a ceramic oven. The result, though, looks quite similar.

WOOD

Christmas decorations are preferably not too figurative for me: no screaming Santas or jolly red-nosed reindeer. I like graphic shapes such as wreaths, pine tree outlines, or the play of stars.

LINEN

Linen string is used to tie packages, but also to wrap gifts in plain instead of festive wrapping paper.

The Christmas balls are in polystyrene foam, covered with strips of linen and burlap.

OUTDOOR

"In the bleak midwinter,
frosty wind made moan,
Earth stood hard as iron,
water like a stone;
Snow had fallen, snow on
snow, snow on snow,
In the bleak midwinter,
long ago."

—CHRISTINA ROSSETTI

The element of fire also comes in handy outside: fire
baskets, a winter barbecue, candles, fireworks . . .
Creating a fairy-tale atmosphere at nightfall.

CREATIVE TIPS

*A few small candles in a windlight, filled with some snow and
mistletoe. Quickly made and always atmosphere-creating.*

*Winter decoration doesn't have to be expensive or chic.
A few flower pots, glass yogurt pots, or a large glass jar
are sufficient.*

*I love making ice decorations. Opposite page: In the photo
to the left, I placed a small can in a large one, then filled the
space between with water, berry branches, and pine greenery.
To the right, I filled the bottom of a yogurt pot with star anise,
pine twigs, and water. I also threaded the string before putting
the ice medallion into the freezer.*

"In every walk with
nature, one receives
far more than he seeks."

–JOHN MUIR

"Lost

Stand still.
The trees ahead and bushes
beside you are not lost.
Wherever you are called Here.
And you must treat it as a
powerful stranger,
Must ask permission to know
it and be known.
The forest breathes.
Listen.
It answers.
I have made this place around you,
If you leave it
You may come back again
Saying . . .
'Here.'
No two trees are the same to raven.
No two branches are the same to wren.
If what a tree or branch does is
lost on you,
You are surely lost.
Stand still.
The forest knows where you are.
You must let it find you."

—DAVID WAGNER

TEXT & STYLING: MARIE MASUREEL

PHOTOGRAPHY:
MARIE MASUREEL
JEROEN VAN DER SPEK: Pages 16, 23, 24, 25, 30, 49, 56, 57, 66 (r), 67, 72, 91 (rb), 98, 99, 109, 121, 131, 134, 139, 144, 145, 148, 149, 155, 161, 168, 175, 185, 188, 189, 190, 200, 202, 203, 205, 210, 212, 213 (lo), 214 (l), 222
SARAH VAN HOVE FOR WONEN LANDELIJKE STIJL: Pages 45, 78, 79, 169, 206 (r)
JAN LIÉGEOIS FOR WONEN LANDELIJKE STIJL: Pages 33 (b), 40, 41, 81, 83, 100, 101, 111, 125, 127, 167 (o), 195, 209
VERNE (VIA MI CASA): Pages 140, 141

GRAPHIC DESIGN: KATRIEN VAN DE STEENE, WHITESPRAY

TRANSLATION (FROM DUTCH TO ENGLISH): MICHAEL LOMAX

TYPESETTING FOR THE RIZZOLI EDITION: JORDAN WANNEMACHER

WITH THANKS TO:
PASCALE NAESSENS, for writing the preface
ANTHRACITE INTERIEURS (www.anthracite.be), BY MOLLE (bymolle.com),
COULEUR LOCALE (www.couleurlocale.eu), GHESQ (ghesq.com),
HOUSE IN STYLE (www.houseinstyle.nl), PURE & ORIGINAL (www.pure-original.com),
PUUR WONEN (www.puurwonensophie.be), VACHT VAN VILT (www.vachtvanvilt.nl),
WALTER VAN GASTEL (www.vangastel.be) for lending material

First published in the United States of America in 2020 by
Rizzoli International Publications, Inc.
300 Park Avenue South
New York, NY 10010
www.rizzoliusa.com

Originally published in Dutch in 2018 as
Sfeervol wonen op het ritme van de natuur by Lannoo Publishers
©2018 Uitgeverij Lannoo nv, Tielt

Printed in Poland
2020 2021 2022 2023 / 10 9 8 7 6 5 4 3 2 1
ISBN: 978-0-8478-6794-3
Library of Congress Control Number: 2019945654

Visit us online:
Facebook.com/RizzoliNewYork
Twitter: @Rizzoli_Books
Instagram.com/RizzoliBooks
Pinterest.com/RizzoliBooks
Youtube.com/user/RizzoliNY
Issuu.com/Rizzoli